STRIDERS

Amazing Animals

Contents

SCHOLASTIC

Published in the UK by
Scholastic Education, 2024
Scholastic Distribution Centre, Bosworth Avenue,
Tournament Fields, Warwick, CV34 6UQ
Scholastic Ireland, 89E Lagan Road, Dublin
Industrial Estate, Glasnevin, Dublin, D11 HP5F

© 2024 Scholastic

1 2 3 4 5 6 7 8 9   4 5 6 7 8 9 0 1 2 3

Printed by Ashford Colour Press

This book is made of materials from
well-managed, FSC®-certified forests
and other controlled sources.

MIX
Paper from
responsible sources
FSC
www.fsc.org   FSC® C011748

A CIP catalogue record for this book is available
from the British Library.

ISBN 978-0702-32731-5

Author
Jilly Hunt

Editorial team
Rachel Morgan, Vicki Yates, Caroline Hale,
Alison Gilbert

Design team
Dipa Mistry, Andrea Lewis and We Are Grace

Photographs
Cover, p10–11, 22 guvendemir/iStock
Cover (background) cornflowerz/Shutterstock
p1, 4, 7, 8, 12, 13, 16, 17, 18, 19, 20, 22, 23
(brush stroke graphic) TMvectorart/Shutterstock
p4 Mongkolchon Akesin/Shutterstock
p5 kyrien/Shutterstock
p5, 21, 24 (background) MG Drachal/Shutterstock
p6 (background) Omeris/Shutterstock
p6 Studio Peace/Shutterstock
p7 Everett Collection/Shutterstock
p8–9 inavanhateren/Shutterstock
p8 (donkey) acceptphoto/Shutterstock
p11 (woman and dog) Photographer and
Illustrator/iStock
p11, 13, 17, 18 (circle) Azindianlany/Shutterstock
p12–13, 23 Wonderful Nature/Shutterstock
p13 (diver and shark) frantisehojdysz/Shutterstock
p14–15, 23 Tommy_McNeeley/iStock
p15 (landscape) Artush/Shutterstock
p16–17 mezzotint/Shutterstock
p17 (dog), 22 K9 and photography/Shutterstock
p17 (skydiver) George Trumpeter/Shutterstock
p18 (fire) MashaSay/Shutterstock
p18–19, 23 Mr. Witoon Boonchoo/Shutterstock
p20 Roman Chazov/Shutterstock
p21, 22 24K-Production/Shutterstock
p22–23 (background) Kimama/Shutterstock
p22–23 (frames) Oleksandr Poliashenko/
Shutterstock

How to use this book

This book practises these letters and letter sounds:

y (as in 'story')	wh (as in 'when')	y (as in 'try')
ow (as in 'show')	ph (as in 'phone')	le (as in 'little')
al (as in 'animal')	c (as in 'celebrates')	ve (as in 'have')
o-e (as in 'some')	se (as in 'house')	ey (as in 'key')
ou (as in 'you')		

Here are some of the words in the book that use the sounds above:

some   animal   owner   immense   when

This book uses these common tricky words:

**are   to   the   they   people   one   of   was
called   their   do   there   into   many**

Before reading

- Read the title and look at the cover. Discuss what the book might be about.

During reading

- If necessary sound out and then blend the sounds to read the word: a-n-i-m-al, animal.
- Pause every so often to talk about the information.

After reading

- Talk about what has been read.
- Use the index on page 24 to select any pages to revisit.

Amazing Animals

Some animals are amazing, thanks to the love they show to people.

This statue celebrates a loyal little dog that protected its owner's grave for 14 years.

Some loyal animals have been given celebratory medals.

One of the first animal medals given was in 1940 to a dog called Fluff. She helped her owners out from the rubble of their house.

Animals on the Battlefield

Some animals show immense bravery on the battlefield.

One donkey's bravery was celebrated with a statue. This army donkey carried wounded fighters from the battlefield to the hospitals.

Army dogs are often fearless in their quest to save lives.

They use their fantastic sense of smell to uncover the enemy or explosives.

In the Wild

We don't understand why some animals help us, but they do. There are amazing stories about dolphins and whales keeping people safe out at sea.

Dolphins have circled around people to protect them from sharks.

Another amazing story is about a group of lions. The group followed the cries of a young girl in trouble and protected her.

When help arrived, the lions quietly left.

Tragically, some animals, like elephants, are at risk from poaching.

A fearless dog called Arrow and his owner tackle poaching in an amazing way. They skydive into remote countryside to try to stop poachers.

Fantastic Helpers

A pet parrot came to the rescue when a fire started in the middle of the night.

He made the sound of the house alarm to wake up his owner.

Service animals are fantastic helpers. They allow their owners to live an independent life.

Service dogs help with key jobs like picking up the phone or dropped money.

Animals can be incredible in many ways.

Which animals do you think deserve to be celebrated? Why?

Index